My Collection, Our Journey

by Tedd

authorHOUSE®

*AuthorHouse*™
*1663 Liberty Drive*
*Bloomington, IN 47403*
*www.authorhouse.com*
*Phone: 1-800-839-8640*

*First published by AuthorHouse    08/22/2011*

*ISBN: 978-1-4634-6808-8 (sc)*
*ISBN: 978-1-4634-6809-5 (ebk)*

*Library of Congress Control Number: 2011915072*

*Printed in the United States of America*

This collection has been a journey into homeless, mental and physical health and self discovery. Like the poems from my older collections, I try more than anything to give you a moment in time. My poems are not about revealing me but revealing you. I try to say here are the moments in time that you might not have been able to express. Or maybe it was a family member or friend who couldn't express it. I hope more than anything you walk away from this collection like you took part of this journey, and that it has enriched, enlighten and empowers you.

Thank you,


Tedd

## The Mask

under covers of sadness
and chemicals
hidden within walls
of protection
do we lay
we lay waiting for
the moment to reawaken
like the blossoms of spring
once the snows of
denial and hibernation
melt away
do we shine in the glory
to show our true
inner beauty
amidst the rugged
weeds and unforgiving
landscape
a piece of splendor
in a world of
ugliness . . .

## Bond of Trust

Trust
a simple word
a simple act
yet complex and fleeting
in the initial moment
of contact
we have the opportunity
to share
for some it is lost
for some found
Trust
once we move
beyond the moment
do we venture into the path
is the bond
worth keeping
or is it worth
taking away
if that bond is
broken can it
be redone
Trust
for something so
simple why
is it such a
key ingredient
in a complex
recipe . . .

## A measure of worth

when we are loss
in a tumbleweed
bouncing and rolling
aimlessly in
a sea of illness
can we
still find the
courage, the wisdom
the strength
to love ourselves
forgive ourselves
and know we
are worth
the time to understand
the power of recovery
the chance to say
I am sorry
we are worth
the opportunity
of a helping hand . . .

Self

a child left alone
to deal in a world
unfamiliar and harsh
to understand how to
survive a sea of emotions
uncharted and unguided
a child left alone
to become a man
loss of innocence yet treasured
and hidden
a child left to self
self is where it stayed
now grown facing a
new world of unfamiliar
and uncharted
scared to abandonment
a knowledge of lifetime
of self to enter a
world of unity and
community yet still
clinging onto self hoping
that is enough . . .

## Miss Thang and Me

Miss Thang and me
two peas in a pond
quiet at first look
but funny wild at heart
once you pass the surface
Miss Thang and me
comforting, joking and dealing
with darkness knowing
the other had our back
to make sure we didn't fall
far
Miss Thang and me
a friendship from the
start
Miss Thang and me
a good thing indeed . . .

## The Trail

a call only a few answer
tugged at my heart
released the ties of the daily grind
to answer the call of freedom
left behind a life unhappy
under my feet the trail
was unforgiving
rocky, steep and rough was she
yet the sense of accomplishment
when reaching the top
and the sweet reward awaiting
to sit on the edge and
breathe in the view surrounding me
to have all of my body sigh
to have a wave of relaxation and home
overtake my body
only to leave early
and leave behind the trail
for a life unsure . . .

## Planned Failure

I and I alone planned this failure
it was simple and easy to do
I did it before I took my
first step, my first breathe
my first actions
I did it without even a
thought or a moment
I did it
I and I alone got me to this place
I did it for reasons known
and unknown
I did it because it was all
that I have known till
this moment
I did not have the knowledge
or faith that there was
a life outside of this
I and I alone planned this failure
because failure was sweeter
and easier to believe than
a life of success . . .

The Promise

I promise
to give myself the opportunity
for the first time to have
a moment to be weak and vulnerable
I promise
to allow myself the experience
for the first time to have
a moment to be whole and loved
I promise
to give myself the acceptance
for the first time to
have a moment to admit
what I know, what I survived
what I have done until
this moment is forgiven, ok
and is in the past for which I
have no control over
I promise
myself today for which
is this moment in which
I can shine as bright as a thousand stars
love a million unconditional loves
the laughter of a child
strength of ten muscle men
wisdom of the ages
and the promise
to myself that all that
I may have to face, I know
I can turn to myself and
those who are now in my life
for the courage and help

to stay in this moment
until tomorrow comes
and becomes today
and when it comes
I promise
to make this promise
again until my
last breathe from
old age and mother nature
this I promise
today a new day
in which to live
and not let myself
be the person I was
but the person I truly
want to be
this I promise . . .

## Unsaid

unsaid, unseen, unknown
is a word balance by a force
so simple yet so complex
a word which has many
shades and colors
a word many learn
to express and deal with
a word for which I can
not say, for it is a word
if I speak means I have
to leave the comfort of
my knowledge and skills
for a life filled with this word
now standing at the crossroads
do I dare speak this word
or do I go back to the safety
and loneliness of a life
without feelings . . .

Walking a Mile

the air
cold and wet from a day brought by fall
the mood
still lifeless decaying like the leaves of a tree
the thought
like many before a repeat of unsaid feelings
the closeness
the room filled with people of different
creeds
the desire
to reach out and express my inner thoughts
the shame
I did not have the courage to open up
the guilt
from not allowing myself the freedom
the feeling
to finally leave the life I know for anew
the wish
to walk a mile in the experiences
that surround me
to know each one of those miles
to share that mile and release
the burden of that mile
so that in turn I could let go
of my mile . . .

## Happy Dance

the music pumping jumping
stirring the air into a frenzy
the pulse shaking moving my
soul to the rhythm and beat
of the music
lifting my soul from its long
winter slumber to awaken
arise anew to melody
to feel my feet and body twist
and shimmy
to let my spirit go free
in the wind and blending
with the happy dance
filling the room . . .

## Who am I Today

This was visited many years ago
yet it has come up again so
Who am I?
I am a man divided into three
a mind, a body, an emotion
Who am I?
a body decaying and broken unnatural
and foreign
filled with pain and joints
twisted, inflamed and cut off
the only thing I can control
is the will to make them move
to get thru the day
Who am I?
an emotion
that is like an iceberg only the
tip to be seen and used as a
beacon in an icy sea of frozen
time, frozen memories, frozen feelings
I try to use the upper part to
make me real and tangible
yet under the surface
is an unconditional love, a love
so great it is one of those loves
of a lifetime, yet it seems I am
unable to release it, express it, share it
it seems only I want it, only I
can survive it, only I understand it
deeper or mixed in is a light
a light so great it can shine
across the globe and bring anyone

out of the darkness
it is a light I have used for
years to keep me going, to help
me out of my own darkness
Who am I?
here is where it gets tricky
Who am I?
a mind, yes a mind
a mind as strong as a diamond
yet as fragile as glass
a mind filled with thoughts
a will to keep going
to get up each day and make it
thru yet another day
where I am going is unknown
unsure and uneasy
yet I go, I will myself
past the pain, over the hurdles of suicide
and depression
a mind stronger than my body or feelings
a mind that now exhausted
wanting to find safety
a chance to see if someone
other me can say
you are worth it, you are loved,
you are needed and allowed
to ask for help
you and you as you is enough
even if it is broken it is still enough
that is who I am?
me . . .

## Walking with the Lord

given up are the worldly possessions
given up the heavy heart of burden
given up the ways of doing things my way
turning my life over
to start to walk the path onto the new
where the path leads
I do not know
renewal of faith is this
there is no failure only success
for this I can say
since walking with the Lord
my soul is fulfilled . . .

## Thanksgiving of Friendship

Thank you for being my friend
I have not expressed this to you
you have been there for the good times
yet I hide the bad times from you
I robbed your friendship and only gave you
half
yet your remained faithful
waiting for me to come out of the darkness
and into the light, to once again rejoice
and be merry
I am so sorry for the moments
I missed and memories not shared
and I wanted to say thank you
for being my friend . . .

## Madness of the mind

In the daily life the voices come
encircling, embracing
surrounding the mind in an entanglement
of madness
reality is broken like a mirror
reflecting upon the mind is a vicious circle
lost in a battle of words
only to be expressed in violence and anger
nothing can reach it, yet only enflame it
life alone out of fear
life alone out of lack of understanding
left alone in the madness of the mind . . .

Empty are the words

once again I am embracing my gift
of poetry
like many times before
empty are the words
write the words I do, but at the point
of almost forcing them out
and not quite enjoying them
the poems seem fine
yet lacking a bit
so once again I will lay down
my pen and wait
for the words not to be empty . . .

## Homeless or Homebound

I know most would think homeless
is a person dirty and unclean,
stuck on the streets with sorrow and pain
caught up in a world of drugs, drinks and
things,
yet since I was a little child I have felt
homeless,
I have finally come to the realization that
homeless is a life without God.

Regardless if you have a job, a home,
money, car, fame you can be homeless and
not know it.
I in all my bareness came face to face with
God, and knew that the two paths before
me
one was me in all of myself survivor, self love,
self awareness and death,
the other was the path of God and to
accept him and let him put the path before
me
and guide my steps.

I finally with a mighty thanksgiving am I
grateful and rejoiceful, that I can finally say
that I am homebound and no longer
homeless,

My prayer now is for you,
that you too may be homebound
and no longer homeless . . .

## A Father's Love

Son,
I knew you before you were here,
I dreamt of you,
I saw your whole life

Son,
then you came into this world and grew
and a whole new world
a whole new life
came true

Son,
you taught me the meaning of a man
you taught me the love of the Lord
you taught me how
to accept and be part of a world
larger than me

Son,
never for a moment's thought
think I do not love you
know I am proud of you, love you
and think the world of you

Son,
thank you for being gay
for it has been a blessing from God . . .

## My Love

my love
even though we have not yet met
my heart belongs to you
I'll be glad and rejoiceful
for the life we have together
for the years of triumph
for the years of tears
my love
my heart sings a song of glory
my soul basks in the warmth of our love
my mind dreams the dreams
that only a dreamer can dream
my love
simple precious love
my love
I give the Lord
praise and glory
for bringing such a great man
in my life
so that I may have a piece
of the Lord's love here on earth
my love
from now to eternity
my love . . .

## Unspoken Love

I've known you since a child
since that time I've wanted
to tell you how much I love you,
but it took me some time
it took a lot of lessons learned
to finally understand
and now express the love
I have for you
sorry for the unspoken love
sorry not letting the love guide me
sorry can't be said enough
I hope I can now find the
words to express the
unspoken love
that I still have in my heart . . .

## Beacon of Love

in the sea of worldly stresses
above the shores of bitterness
sits a beacon of love
bright enough to pierce any storm
and melt any soul that see it's brilliance
a beacon of love
to guide the lost and the lonely
to comfort the hurt and the weak
a beacon of love
a way home unto the Lord
a beacon of love
that can be shared
and passed on like a torch
igniting a new beacon
so that love
can grow and reach new heights
to one day the love of the Lord
can be truly seen
in everyone and in everything . . .

## A prayer for others

I pray for you
I do not know
I pray for you
in case no one else is there to pray for you
I pray for you
so that you may know the love
I pray for you
that you may be blessed
I pray for you
that your heart be opened
that you see the glory of the Lord
that you may know
I prayed for you
so I pray for you
because you prayed for me
and I know . . .

The wind

with each breeze
my souls opens
the cool gentle touch
I feel him in it
helping me release my sorrow
letting me rejoice in this day
guiding my thoughts into the light
with each breeze
my soul opens
and I rejoice and praise his name
with each breeze
I'm renewed
and thankful for it . . .

## Conflict with man of this world

forgive me father
for I can no longer
stay quiet while men of this world
preach that being gay is a sin
being saved means
you used to be gay
now you have to be straight
you love me father
you loved me before the
men of this world said it
was evil and a sin
it was the men of this world
that added it to your word
I will no longer listen to
them and let their
polluted ways taint
my heart
I am walking away from
them
please forgive me
and bless them for they
do not understand your love
for me . . .

You matter

two little words
written on a brown paper bag
inside a simple sandwich
cookies, crackers, a piece of fruit
two little words
that someone took the time
to write, sitting at home
making a meal for someone
two little words
that some might over look
yet some take notice that
someone took the time
to make a simple meal
and say
you matter . . .

## A Supermodel
*(random thought not completely a poem)*

I know I have posted pics of hot supermodels. The guys we like to fantasy. For those who are straight just insert a hot female supermodel. These guys have the body we wish we all could have. And eyes we get lost in. We wonder did they get the manual? Did they understand it better than we did? Did they have someone show them the manual or were they just lucky enough to find it?

Sometimes I wonder if I had the manual, what would have I done differently if anything at all. If at childhood I was not abandon and made fun of, would my life be the same. Would it be better or worse? They tell us that you can't be happy, you can't love until you love yourself and are happy with yourself. Well what happens when over the course of time you sacrificed a piece here and a piece there. Gave up one dream for a lesser. What if after years of self happiness and self love, you don't have any left. What if who you are is like your faded memory, just a fuzzy moment in time. The details aren't clear, you sort have a happy thought, you sort of see the faces and the moment, but like all things lost, weathered in time.

I do have consider myself lucky. I haven't done drugs, or become an alcoholic or smoked. I got to have two long term relationships. I got to see most of the United States. I gone on cruises and trips and have done some things most would only dream about and not have the courage to do. I have boldly gone sometimes head first into deep uncharted waters. Scared at times, happy at times and in the end have learned alot and have met alot of people. Some who I have changed their lives and some who have changed mine.

I have never been what some would call good looking or a catch. I always wanted to be a super model to be admire and fantasized about. Yet like all things they are just pictures on a piece of paper. In some small way I am a supermodel. I just haven't found my magazine. In an odd way that is ok, because for all of my quirks and flaws, I am flesh. I am not just a glossy piece of paper. Yet, I wish that I had taken a chance or a moment to capture who I was, for now I have nothing left to remind myself of the bold, unique supermodel, who just happened to be before their time and before there was a magazine for them. I happen to be like so many others, a lost cover spread in the fabric of time. A supermodel forever young and forever lost in a faded memory.

## Alone on a beach

it was a warm sunny summer day
the breeze was cool, refreshing and inviting
as I strolled the park
I saw it
a little patch of sun amidst the trees
I got my blanket out
removed my shoes and socks
and laid in the sun
I closed my eyes
as the hush of the waves
crash along the beach
my mind drifted away
as the stress oozed away
as wave after wave passed by
alone on a beach
on a quiet summer's day . . .

## Words for this moment

I wish I knew the words
I wish I could express
the emotion at this moment
I wish I knew what emotion
it was
I wish I had the words
to tell you I am sorry
for not seeing you
I know that in my mind
you didn't see me
yet was I seeing you
was I giving you credit
was I giving you your moment
I wished I was invisible
and it seems I am
I wish I didn't hurt so much
yet was the hurt self inflicted
I wish I knew the words
for this moment . . .

Love

if you really didn't know
emotions
could you still love?
could you be capable of loving
yourself or others
I see love around me
I think I have it inside of me
yet do I?
can love be beyond emotions
or does it need emotions to live
after years of pain and suffering
can one still love?
or is love too precious of a thing
to live in a man
with a mind full of madness . . .

When is enough, enough

at what part do we get the right to say
enough!
how much pain does it need to weigh
how much suffer does it have to endure
how many years
or does one never have the right to say
enough!
is that the one word we do not speak
of? why?
is it because of fear or envy
is it because we ask that ourselves
when is enough, enough? . . .

The maddening layers of pain

pop
like the fireworks on a hot fourth of july
pop
pop
pop, aaaeee
like the fireworks on a hot fourth of july
like a southern banshee screaming
from a snow capped mountain top
pop
pop
pop, aaaeee
pop, aaaeee
pop, aaaeee, voosh
like the fireworks on a hot fourth of july
like a southern banshee screaming
from a snow capped mountain top
like a spinning twirl a derby in a
side show carnival
pop, aaaeee
pop, aaaeee
pop, aaaeee, voosh
pop, aaaeee, voosh
pop, aaaeee, voosh, pop, kaboom
like the fireworks on a hot fourth of july
like a southern banshee screaming
from a snow capped mountain top
like a spinning twirl a derby in a
side show carnival
like the fireworks on a hot fourth of july
like an echoing thunder from
a heat storm shaking the earth and air

pop, aaaeee, voosh
pop, aaaeee, voosh
pop, aaaeee, voosh, pop, kaboom
pop, aaaeee, voosh, pop, kaboom
pop, aaaeee, voosh, pop, kaboom, ererekkk
like the fireworks on a hot fourth of july
like a southern banshee screaming
from a snow capped mountain top
like a spinning twirl a derby in a
side show carnival
like the fireworks on a hot fourth of july
like an echoing thunder from
a heat storm shaking the earth and air
like the sharp fingernails of steel
scrapping against a blacken chalk board
pop, aaaeee, voosh, pop, kaboom
pop, aaaeee, voosh, pop, kaboom
pop, aaaeee, voosh, pop, kaboom, ererekkk
pop, aaaeee, voosh, pop, kaboom, ererekkk
these are just a few of
the maddening layers of pain
which I must endure
each second of a minute . . .

## Path of Forgiveness

rocky
dark dim stumbling amidst the rocks and
bushes
clawing
using the last bit of strength to climb back up
the hill
scared
seeing the distance beneath and the
crumbling rocky fall
racing
the heart pounding the sweat making it hard
to hold on
stumbling
you lose your grip reaching out for
anything, something
relief
a branch slightly dead but just may be
strong enough
climbing
again finding a stone to hold onto to push
yourself up
surprise
upon the realization you made it to the top
fear
once you realize the surroundings are
deserted
chard, burnt and decayed
struggle
you start to walk forward unknown where
you are walk to
joy
a sign faded, old barely noticeable saying

"next gas station 2 miles"
determined
desperate the thirst from the dry air
the blisters that are now your feet
walking
amidst the decaying, the death swelters
puzzled
you come to the gas station only to see a
sign
"all may passage once forgiven"
forgiveness
who do we forgive or do we need to be
the one who needs forgiven
enlighten
a thought, a simple thought like a whisper
in the air
it is ok to forgive
you survived the trials
you endured the tests
it is now time to forgive
yourself for it was not your fault
and forgive others
for they too may be lost in the
desert still searching for their way
forgive
I forgive myself for I am worth
more than negative words
I forgive others for they too have suffered
from those same negative words
and no one ever told them
they are forgiven and
worth more than the negative words
they were told time and again . . .

Letter of forgiveness

dear self
I forgive you
I am sorry I didn't love you
and protect you when you were
weak and scared
dear family
I forgive you
I am sorry I could not be all
that you wanted me to be
dear friends
for not giving you a chance
for not understanding what
a friend was
dear self
to my inner child
please forgive me for not
telling you are worth more
that you are beautiful
strong, caring and unique
a child who I would
like to heal
dear self
I am finally ready to say
I love you . . .

worth

we are worth
more than money
more than self image
more than harsh criticisms
we are worth
a moment
a moment to let down
the walls of protection
a moment to be vulnerable
silly, joyful, loving, caring
we are worth
beyond any artificial or superficial
thing we can produce
we are worth
a moment
to be more than a label
a past full of mistakes
we are worth
a moment
filled with hope
filled with compassion
and we are worth
a moment
to know we have
worth . . .

this is me

it is small and meek
almost a ghost of a faded memory
it is just a seed
at this point not sure what is
real and what is fantasy
but this is me
batter, bruised, beaten
forgotten and lost
yet in the dark is a ball of hope
where lives the love to make
others smile
a place where I can dream
the impossible dreams
where I am attractive
I am lovable and I am
more than a throw rug
this is me
sometimes shy and unseen
but sometimes a glimpse
a moment comes by
where I can let it be free
and show the kindness
and love that I have to offer
underneath the wall of invisibility . . .

My gift to you

dear friend
even though we have not met
or there may be miles between us
I am giving you this gift
the gift is a ball
in this ball is all the hope
you need to survive another day
all the light you need to get
thru the darkness
all the armor needed to defend
against the harsh words
all the dreams to lift
you up to reach the stars
and a mirror to show you
the inner beauty you have
beneath all of the scars
bruises, hurt and ugliness that surrounds
you
I am giving you this gift
unconditional with no strings
or obligations
the ball has all the energy
to last a day to a decade
please accept this gift
love your friend
me . . .

## the release of bondage

when it started, how it started
or why it started
no long matters
they are now just faded memories
part real part fantasy
but the chains of bondage
you are in today need to be
released
there is no one to blame
there is no one to forgive
there is only you
and starting today
I am giving you permission
to empower yourself
to yourself
to let go of the bondage
its safety only cuts deeper
its hold only get stronger
it is time to allow yourself
to cry, to love, to be vulnerable
and to ask for help
you have the permission
to release the bondage
and enjoy life . . .

## seeing the unseen

you felt like a mirror
only projecting what others wanted
to see
yet
you comforted those who needed
comforted
you brought smiles to those
whose days were dark
you made someone feel special
and beautiful when they thought
no one noticed them
you took the courage when
others said you will fail
and took the challenge
it may not have gone
the way you wanted
but along the way you
learned even more about
yourself and others
so now is the time
to see the unseen
and see how empowered
you are and how
kind, loving and caring
all the things that are most
important of all . . .

embracing the moment

it is ok for you to be scared
hurt, anxious, angry, confused
lost, trapped, feeling like a failure
they are all real feelings
embrace them
see them for what they are
a moment
one simple moment
take the moment to let it out
then let the moment go
embrace a new moment
where it is filled with acceptance
with joy, happiness
achievement and releasing
of the past
for that moment has past
the future moment is not
to be worried about
enjoy this moment
let it empower you
strengthen you
and renew your soul
live for this moment
so it can make the next moment
even better . . .

one word

if I could say one word
it would be
hello
hello to your inner beauty
hello to your inner joy
hello to your inner empowerment
hello
I see you and just wanted
to say
hello
my name is
me . . .

## vulnerability of scars

we feel we have to hide our scars
some are physical
some are mental
some are emotional
some scars fade
some scars remain
but of hiding them, no
show them
do not be afraid of them
because having the scar
means one thing
you survived
you lived thru it
and are still here
and can be an inspiration
to someone else
who may have a similar
scar
and afraid they may not
make it
let your scar be a mark of
beauty, instead of a mark
of shame . . .

you are forgiven

if you are lost in the darkness
if you are lost in the sea of anxiety
if you are locked in the prison of your mind
I am giving you permission
to forgive yourself
to forgive others
and the permission to say
I am forgiven
this is your key
this is your pass
this is your time
to be free
to come to safety
heal the wounds
let the heart rejoice
and let the burden of your soul
free
for you are forgiven
and that is all that matters . . .

## my battle

I know it took me a long time
to get here
I am still not sure of what lies ahead
and if I still have the strength
for my battle
but I will remember this much
I am still here
I don't know if all of the
wounds will heal
or if I will ever be completely
whole
but I know that I have
survived this far
alone and with no help
I now have been
told that I have always
had the tools to win this
battle I just needed
to know how to use them
so I will now face this
battle knowing I have
what it takes to win it
and be victorious . . .

blossoms of spring

fall has come
and soon winter
but after the harshness
comes the blossoms of spring
the sweet fragrance filling
the air
bringing new life
bringing new beauty
with the blossoms of spring
comes the renewal of life
and all of the love
and the joy and splendor
nature has to offer
with the blossoms of spring
comes the uplifting of the soul
to inspire new dreams
new songs
new beginnings
so remember with the
falling of leaves and the icy breeze
of winter, will dawn
the blossoms of spring . . .

pedals of our heart

like a rose bud our heart starts
slowly opening
pedal by pedal
to soon the rose is
fully blossom
the fragrance is overpowering
memories of romance and love
fill the air
then slowly the pedals
fade away
fall to the ground
and become a seed
all we have to do is
is wait till harshness
goes away and again
we will become a
new rose bud
this time with more
shades of beauty
and a new fragrance
that entices new memories
and new loves . . .

empowered

I am no longer invisible
I am no longer the blame
I am no longer ugly or fat
I am me
I am empowered
I will shine
I will love
I will heal
and I will give you
a second chance
a chance to be part of this
new life
because I wanted to share
my empowerment
so that you to know
that you are beautiful
that you are brave
that you are strong
and you mean the world
to me
so friend let us now
empower ourselves
and enjoy life to the fullest . . .

failure to see

I failed to see for many
years now that I did not
belong in this world
it didn't matter how many
poems I wrote they will
never change anyone's life
it didn't matter now
many homes I designed
I would never have one
it didn't matter sex
came naturally to me
because it did not give me
the only thing I wanted
affection, intimacy, love
it didn't matter how
hard I worked to be
the perfect person
caring, giving, loving
friendship, inspiring
it didn't matter
how much abuse I
endure
it didn't matter how
hard I pushed by body
beyond its limits
I failed to see that I
didn't belong in this
world
that the love
the endless, boundless
unconditional love

was not enough
and the light I had
was not strong enough
to save those in
the darkness
I fail to see
I was not enough
I wasn't strong enough
brave enough
handsome enough
worthy enough
I failed to
see that me
and the world
would never mixed
I am sorry for my failure
please forgive me
I hope now
you and I can find peace
and maybe someday
someone would see
my poetry, my homes
and realize the
power they had
I am just sorry
I failed to be me
and not the me
the world wanted me to be
forgive me . . .

## To be human

what makes us human
is it emotions
is it faith in the unseen
is it a connection to others
to be human
is my quest
right now I feel like
a speck of dust
floating in the wind
if I fly or fall seems
not to matter
to be human
is the first step
to strip ourselves
of us for who we are
and accept ourselves
for the good, bad and in-between
to be human
to be human
do I have the voice
to say, yes I am human
I am me
and that is all that matters . . .

## Restabilizing

I am going so fast
I am not seeing the danger signs
I am not seeing the outreach hands
I am not seeing the help
I am in a fog
my mind lost forgotten
yet like a racing locomotion
train falling off a cliff
impulsive
running
scared
lost
yet here I am again
in the dark but this
time I feel safer
this time I know I have
to make it work
I have to get out of the
darkness
and come back to life
come back into the light
and restabilize . . .

## Ode to Aneka

she like a guardian angel
held out her hand
kept it out there in the darkness
for me to grab onto
she saw the light
the beauty
the good in me
she tried so hard for
me to see it
yet I failed her and me
I failed because
I was unable to accept
me
I was unable to see
me
she had faith in me
she had light for me
and all I can say
now is I am sorry
and thank you
I hope I am not too late
I hope I can finally
accept me
and make both of us proud
me accepting me
and doing for myself
is probably the best gift
and only gift
I can give her
so this is my Ode to Aneka
I am doing this for

me
me, I said it
me
I am Tedd
I am human
I am love
I am light
I will shine
I will get thru
the darkness
this is my Ode to Aneka
my guardian angel
I am so grateful
you came into my
life . . .

My plan

Step one
enjoy this moment
and make the best of it
Step two
love myself, be true to me
Step three
no longer hide the truth
be not afraid to say
what is really going on inside
Step four
reach out to others they
have a story, they may have a key
they may need a friend
just like you
Step five
look in the mirror
see beyond the image
and see the inner
beauty and hold onto it
Step six
when the storm comes
stand still, take a moment to think
and then make my next move
Step seven
see the small accomplishments
they are just as important
as the big ones
Step eight
stop, drop, and breath
remember to breathe

Step nine
seek out new dreams
make new goals
keep to the plan
Step ten
hang in there even when
you are drowning hang in there
Step eleven
smile, shine, laugh
have fun the good
always outweighs the bad
you have a choice
choose the positive
let go of the past
what's done is done
don't worry about tomorrow
it's not here yet
live in today
Step twelve
refer back to step one
enjoy this moment
and make the best of it
that is most important
of all . . .

the fun of rebuilding

the fun of rebuilding
is the fact you are
able to destroy the past
destruct it, let it go
start from scratch
take one step
one room at a time
what do you want it to feel like
what color do you want
it to be like
once you let go of
the sinking ship
and stand on the beach
take a moment to
let the warm moist
sand rub in between
your toes
enjoy the sound of the waves
take time to smell the fresh sea air
take time to see the
beauty around you
it is time to rebuild
this time make the
most of it
build a strong foundation
and make sure
your home expresses you
the real you
be good to yourself
and others will too . . .

## sea of strangers

a sea of strangers
sharing a meal
some keep quiet to themselves
some laugh
a sea of strangers
brought together by
a common bond
all lost in a sea
of uncharted waters
looking for a safe harbor
looking for a friend
looking to find someone
who shares a common
bond with
a sea of strangers
each finding themselves . . .

## Miss Missy

what can you say about
Miss Missy
she is the embodiment
of a big sister, mother
friend, guardian angel
all rolled up into one
curvy package
Miss Missy
she is the wonder
of Christmas and joy
she has the ability
to reach into the darkness
into you and turn on
your inner beauty
your inner light
your inner self
Miss Missy
she is one of those
unsung heroes you hear
about and I have been
honored and luckily
enough to have her
come into my life twice
Miss Missy
this one is to you
to let you know
how thankful and grateful
and honored I am
to have met you
Miss Missy . . .

## My Choice

it is mine
not others but mine
it is my choice
to what I do with
my life what I do with today
it is my choice
to let the past
tear me apart or to
finally see it for what
it is the past
it is my choice
if all I do is get up
take a shower
go for a walk
eat, each in itself are
small accomplishments
because I choose do them
it is my choice
as to who I am
I can choose to
stay stuck in the past
in the darkness or
I can finally
come into the light
and find out what happiness
feels like
and I am going
to finally exercise
my right to say it is
my choice . . .

## A son's forgiveness

like a ghost haunting
my spirit, I could
never let him out of my mind
I fought foolishly
for so many years
not to look like you
be like you
a ghost haunting me
never giving me a
chance to grieve
to cry, to laugh
to love
now I have finally
reached a point
I can now look in
the mirror and see me
I can now look at
you and not see me
we are now two separate
people
I am finally able to close
the door
and forgive . . .

## A Christmas wish

I wish for you
that in the dark
of the season
may you see the
wonder, joy, love
of the season
may your heart be
warmed
may your mind be
child like
may you see the
world in a new
and wondrous way
my Christmas wish
is for you
may you accept it
and be merry for it . . .

## A photograph of season

a photo of me
inserted with loves lost
family unknown, friends missed
a photo old yet still glossy
underneath lies the truth of
the photo
the unspoken moments,
the buried words and scars of wounds
still fresh
the photo like a leaf
upon my tree
stuck in the season of fall
an eternal fall
clinging on in a photo
I let my friend the wind, come
and let the photo drift away
into the sands of time
as soon as it fades
the avalanche of winter
overwhelms me
I'm frightened and scared
yet now I find comfort
in winter's womb
for when spring comes
for when the dawn arises
so shall I
I will be stronger, wiser
and richer

for now I can let in
the joy, the love and
the life
flow from my heart
a new photo
to reflect the struggle,
the endurance, and the triumph
of my soul
now basking in the light
of today with hope
of a brighter tomorrow . . .

Our journey

this detour of grief was long
and harsh
this road of forgiveness has been
rough and rocky
yet along the way has been
moments of kindness,
acts of family
loves of simple times gone by
our journey
may have taken different
turns and twists
yet our lessons are learned
our hearts renewed
and our stories shared
separate and unique
our journey ends and begins
a crossroad
a new choice to make
a new journey
to search for, may we
continue and
find again . . .

## Love and you

love has been the subject of ages
it is the longing we inspire for
fight for, die for and live for
yet what is love
and why is it so fleeting
is love conditional or is
it forged into an unbreakable
and boundless bond
love needs only one thing
you
with you love sparks
love grows
you are the rock upon
which the kite of
life is tied upon
you ground it
and keep
it from flying too far into
the heavens and becomes lost
among the clouds
so may love be with you
may love start with you
may love have life
in you . . .

poems of old

a life reflect in words
moments saved from
the sands of time
emotions caught
and explained
a life shared
the poems change with
age, grow from simple
to now more complex
and personal
yet now it is a race
against a new foe
for now words are
fleeting
emotions are lost
and time is erased
into a film of dementia
my poems of old
my poems of you
my legacy on paper
etched upon the grains
of memory
leaving me
and living
within you . . .

## My pasture

a life of struggle
and suffering
a life long and strong
now I wait for
my time to come
to have my sense
of peace
to leave the wilds
of the world
for the serenity
of rolling hills
where I can be free
with no expectations
or roles
free to shine
free to be silly
free from a world unknown
and demanding
time to leave
and roam
my pasture . . .

## A chapter closed

even though the journey
is far from over
I feel the ending of this
chapter fast approaching
my heart is closing up shop
my mind is at easy
it feels like the right
time to move on
to begin a new chapter
to tell a new story
I am grateful when looking
back and how lucky
my story did not end
in another way
the bad could have been
much worse
the best was sweeter
than I realized
and in the end I realize
these moments
I have
shared with you
are moments you've
given to me
and I say
"Thank you" . . .

# A measure of a year

when taking stock of this year
this journey, this search
how fortunate am I
I know I have cursed, praised
walked away from, and prayed
to the Lord
I have mostly played neutral
between the tug a war of
good and evil
I know I have gained
much with a better understanding
of myself and all the
people who've come into my life
I have struggled
I have fallen
I have been superhuman
and vulnerable
and intimate
I have gone thru many stages
and have burnt many bridges
opened many wounds
yet been giving a soul
renewed
a year
some would disagree with
yet a year
I would do all
over again . . .